To Clive

With Love

Mary.

(Christmas 1980)

WITH LOVE

WITH LOVE
Richard Beckinsale

Foreword by Judy Beckinsale

FREDERICK MULLER LIMITED
LONDON

W ITH GRATEFUL acknowledgements to Margaret and Arthur Beckinsale, Sally Crampton (Thames Television), Lisette Fairley (London Express News & Feature Services), Alan Parker, Emlyn Price, Ben Rice, Hugh Ross, Philip Wimhurst (Film Distributors Ltd) and Vera Woolf.

First published in Great Britain 1980
by Frederick Muller Limited, London, NW2 6LE

ISBN 0 584 10387 5

Picture credits: BBC TV (p. 67), Black Lion Films (pp. 28, 65 and 68), Euston Films, *Reveille* (p. 31), Scope Features (p. 57) and Thames Television (pp. 34, 41, 46, 55, 73 and 76).

Photoset by D. P. Media Limited, Hitchin, Hertfordshire

Printed in England by Biddles Ltd., Guildford, Surrey.

FOREWORD

I FEEL A LITTLE as I did when, in November 1977, I watched nervously as Richard was ensnared into the *This is Your Life* programme, knowing that, without my assent, he would never have been subjected to what might have been an embarrassing ordeal; a considerable responsibility! I ultimately found, as I had hoped, that many people benefited from that night – his family and friends through their pride and love for him; the public generally, delighted to know a little more about the private person who as an actor they had always cared for – and, not least, Richard himself, who, to his own astonishment, enjoyed and was rewarded by a thoroughly happy evening.

For some time I have been collecting, and also discovering, some of the things that Richard had written. I feel at pains to underline that his aspiration was not as a writer. Richard searched generally for the purest, simplest, most truthful form of communication, and at certain times, invariably emotionally charged ones, this happened to be through the written word. The expression of feeling was the priority; its merit entirely irrelevant. For me to take spontaneous poems and fragments written throughout various stages of his life and share them with a wider audience, irrespective of their private purpose, or whether in his own opinion some of them might merely be discarded jottings, recalls the feelings of responsibility I suffered in 1977. And yet, I feel, as I did then, that people might benefit and that Richard might not entirely have disapproved.

Richard, in an interview, once said, 'I've always had this desire to communicate a great kind of beauty to other people, to transport people to the world where I live . . . to give people love, to teach people love. I think it is probably the main driving force in my life.'

Love, and the joy and pain of trying to 'catch a sunbeam' are basically the themes running through his writing. The Reverend John Arrowsmith at the 'Celebration' service held for Richard at St. Paul's Church, Covent Garden, said, 'Everyone from close friends to casual acquaintances has used the word "love" when talking about Richard. He had this great capacity to inspire affection. I have never experienced anything quite like it.' He had summed up what had been the common theme of the hundreds of extraordinary letters I received after Richard's death. People who, having described him as 'natural, kind and gentle' and possessing 'a marvellous innocence' and a 'rare and precious gift of making people laugh', went further:

'He inspired a feeling of deep emotion which is hard to explain except that it felt like losing someone very close. I've felt sadness before at the loss of other great stars but never like this.'

'He was like a very good close friend to us, coming into our homes and being regarded as the lovable boy-next-door or one's favourite cousin with whom one had an extra special relationship.'

'He shed so much light and joy it is astonishing.'

'I would like you to know how very much we all loved him.'

'No one will ever fill the hollow he has left, but he brought such happiness to so many, he will never be forgotten.'

'Richard was the light at the end of the tunnel. . . . He will not only be greatly missed as an actor but as a genuine person with love in his heart.'

From Jack Rosenthal, writer of *The Lovers*: 'Among total strangers who'd never even met Richard . . . it's as though they've lost someone they loved, who'd made them happy . . . if love could bring someone back, he'd be back tomorrow.'

Richard never realised quite how much people responded to what someone described as his 'special kind of magic', or to what extent, over and above mere talent and technique, he had communicated that essence of life and love that was most important to him. I feel that some of that 'magic' is in his writing. If only a few respond, it is worthwhile.

Richard, recounting the time he played *Hamlet* in repertory, said, 'I'm sure that ninety-nine per cent of the audience didn't know what was going on. But there was one man right at the back of the theatre who happened to be a vicar and he wrote me a letter afterwards. He knew what was going on, and for me that was enough. He said he wished he could communicate his belief in Christ as strongly as I had communicated my emotions to him on the stage. That was probably the biggest thrill I have ever had – it was the best reaction I could possibly wish for.'

With all those who think and have thought of Richard 'with love' I should like to share this book.

Judy Beckinsale

TRIBUTE

RICHARD USED TO make me laugh a lot.
Although he had the face of a cherubic choirboy,
inside was the soul of a comedian. He loved the con-
tinuing joke, the running gag: he would often quote
odd lines and jokes from previous productions he had
worked in. They would pop up whenever they could
be made to fit the occasion; and of course, as I got to
know them, I would be expected to take part in the
cross-talk. 'Let's do the last scene,' the director would
say.

'Ah,' Richard would reply. 'The Codicil.'

'The what?' I would say.

'The Codicil.'

'What's the codicil?'

'The End bit.'

'How do you spell it?'

'E-N-D-B-I-T.'

These lines were rattled off as a sort of ritual – it
amused us both to hear them repeated. Sometimes it
would be varied slightly:

'How do you spell it?'

'E-N-D-B-T.'

'What happened to the I?'

'It came out in the conversation.'

This referred to another favourite joke: 'I didn't
know she had a glass eye, but it came out in the
conversation.' Richard actually gave me a sort of fake
glass eye once. I still have it, though I can't remember
where he said he got it from. Jokes about eyes seemed
to occur quite frequently: 'Morning, butcher, can I

have a sheep's head – and leave the eyes in, and it will see me through the week.' This old favourite, no doubt from some panto or other that Richard had appeared in, was guaranteed to bring a chuckle to his lips and a twinkle to his eye. Any mention of age on my part would invariably bring the response, 'You're not old. You *look* old, mind you,' followed by the familiar giggle.

Richard loved a good laugh. When I heard that he had died, of course, I cried. Everybody who knew him did. But while writing these few words in affectionate memory of an all too brief friendship, I must admit that I've been laughing again – just thinking about him.

Ronnie Barker

W HEN I WAS a small boy, my main ambition in life was to catch a sunbeam.

If you hold out your hand and let a shaft of sunlight rest on the palm of your hand, you are half-way to capturing it. To make it yours, you have to wrap your hand into a fist, keeping the sunshine inside. You have to be very quick because the sunbeam always seems to manage to jump out of your hand and sit on your knuckles. I have never ever seen it done, but I have seen many people all but catch one. It seems that sunshine is the one thing a man cannot catch.

He catches water and air and mountains and clouds and birds and fish and people and darkness – darkness being the most easy thing to catch. You can even catch darkness when you can't see it. Just hold out your hand and close it quickly, and inside is darkness. But it escapes easily when you open your hand fully. If you peep through your fingers though, you will be able to see some of it left; but don't open your hand too much or away it goes.

I have heard, but I don't know whether it's true or not, that you can catch sunbeams sometimes if you first capture some human love. To catch human love, you have to have tremendous patience because you have to wait for it to come along. You cannot find it ever if you look for it. You also have to have an assistant to help you. There is a great shortage of assistants in the world, and a lot of people cash in on this fact and masquerade as assistants. You have to be very careful because if you get hold of one of these impostors, it can make you really incredibly unhappy. I have heard that it's even enough to make the most ardent sunbeam-catcher give up his task and take up the incredibly easy job of catching the darkness. I think though that I have always been and always will be a sunbeam-catcher. And I will keep on whatever happens.

If I do catch one, I promise I will show it to you and perhaps, if you would like it, help you to catch one for yourself.

Through muddy streets and black canals
Of the dark ages
Of my live long youth
I run so fast
Run away and hide
In dreams of promised futures.

Jumping through the air
With a heart pumping with a love
In creeping autumnal night time
Down Derby Road hill
To catch the 12.50 5b to Beeston
Pulling green privet from hedges
Greener than before
Looking up with tear filled
Joy filled eyes
Brighter than before
At star filled night skies
Closer than before
Breathing cold fresh
Autumn air
Blowing from taxi ranks
And council steps
And unmanned hotdog stalls
Smelling sweaty beer stained
Odours from Yates' Wine Lodge
And the Bell grinning
With closed jaws
From either end of a zebra crossing gangplank
He knew the joy of pure love
He knew not yet the agony of pure pain.

Yesterday was pig day
But that's all gone
Yesterday was someone else's fault
But now I'm the one

Yesterday I'd be hurt
And then forget it
Yesterday I picked my nose
And then I ate it

Now I just pick
The tatty headed Herberts
Who jumped into my scene
The ones who only came and went
But I'll always know they've been.

I'm walking down the highway of the
place I'm supposed to be
but somehow I'm not touching any roadway

Smashed lifeless onto the rocks
Of my own tormented minds
Gashed lifeless by the crashing sea
Of doubt and uncertainty
I am driftwood
Without strength
Without will
Without direction
I fight the first and last fight
On the side of my enemy.
Come sea, bring death quickly
I tear open the flesh
Of my silent screaming neck
For you
Lick the streaming wound with your tongue
Of salt
Sting me with pain unbearable
I am yours to take
Come rocks of a million lifetimes
Crush my bones to dry white dust
Smash my skull into a thousand
Senseless pieces
And throw it against the wind
I am yours rocks
I am yours to break
I am yours sea
I am yours to take
Take me break me
Take me make me
Die
Die now.

A Poem of Hopefulness. . . .
       Come she will . . . one day

One day I will meet her
The phantom floating softly
In my every daydream
Touch and taste
Her every movement
Find myself
In every fold
Of her cool white
Flesh
Live slowly
In the passionate fire
Of her eyes
Dissolve warmly
In the soft calm
Of her voice
Who is she
My serenity
My calm
My peace of all peace
Oh God! Let me discover
Recognise
And hold fast
With strong hands
The crimson glow
Of her love
My pumping heart
Bursts with a power
Unknown and unused
Let it all be gentleness
And peace.

With love . . . R

He's under my moonbeam
And
It makes no difference
Where the alley cat sleeps
One eyed Mowgli of
The back yard
One eared jackal
Of the dustbins
Flea bitten Uncle Tom
Ragbag rat cat
Fish chopped boot buffer
Rhubarb patch carol singer
He catch the feather breath
Sparrow He kill the feather
Throat bluebird He never
Snatched a swallow flying
Insect catcher summer
Blue sky sunshine bird
Ever
But it makes no difference

Scarecrow in The Wizard of Oz: *Crewe, Christmas 1968*

Red is the petal
of your rose
that blows and bends
inside my breast
The rose that lives
inside me
Flower clutched
on crimson stem
that feeds on
love requited
Grow my flower
Make him strong
never let him
cut them.

Maybe I should start
From the top and work down
Cause this bottom to top
Is somehow the wrong way round

My rainbow is a many sided shadow
Swamping through the ruins of my mind
Take a wrong turn down the track
Find the rainbow turned to black
Twist the knife blade in my back
And watch the blood flow.
Turn on the light sweet lady
Let me look on brightening sky
Through the sunshine in your eye
And see my love grow.
When hares run free and mindless
When the martin eats the flies
Let me look into your eyes
And see your rainbow
Through the teardrops of my gladness
I see the fragments of joy
That could rest in sweet awareness
Of your love.
With my outstretched hand I speak
Inside your light mine is weak
Help me find the light I seek.
And see my rainbow
With my rainbow in the shadow
Cast your sunbeams down on me
Fill my shadow with the colours
Of your love. And let me be
Complete with coloured rainbow
Of my own.

*To Judy – the only person I want
to love, the only person I want.*

I want
to stop feeling sick
on the top of buses
I want
to go to Iceland
I want
to be able to
write a cheque for
a thousand pounds
and know it won't
bounce
I want
to believe
in God
I want
Alan Meadows
and
Valerie Georgeson
to have a
baby daughter
I want
to roll cigarettes
that don't
go out
I want
to find happiness
in the present
I want
to be able to
wear contact lenses
all day
I want
my mother
to pass her
driving test

I want
peace and freedom
for all the frightened
people in the world
I want
my father
to be able to
hear what I'm saying
I want
to be able to
drink ten pints of beer
and walk home
on my own
I want
to look in a mirror
and not see myself
I want
to be able
to swim
I want
to die
when I am fifty-four
years old
I want
not to be
lazy
I want
to marry you
I want
a dog
I want
to die
in your arms
I want
you
to always be the sunshine.

Take me down
Take me down
Sweet lady of the sunlight
Take me down and
Let me drink
The sweetness of the brook
Let me drink
The water clear
Of morning sun and starlight
Guide me out
Into the stream
That I may slake my thirst.

Don't let the angel fly
Through your fingers
Don't let him fly blindly
Into the wall of nowhere
He may fly close to the sun.

Part of an anthology. . . .
To be spun on Summer moonbeams.

Dream
Of silver shadows
Walk in moonlight
Floating softly
Near me

Try to catch the
Misty movement
Bring it closely
To me

Try to give my
Dream a name
Know it keep it
Always

Try to give my
Dream a face
Honest eyes that
See me

Try to give my
Dream a voice
Talking softly
To me

Dream
Of silver shadows
Walk in moonlight
Floating softly
Past me.

With love. . . R

27

One of these nights
You're going to wake up
Screaming
For a hand to put on the light
For arms to take you
And hold your shaking body
Close to his heartbeat
And soothe you out of fear
Of your hysterical nightmare

In your dream you saw pain
And hunger
Death and disease
Fire and torture
And torment unceasing

In your head you saw blood
Of little children
Of many men
And women of your own
Splashed and drenched
In steaming crimson
You ran away from your own mind
On the feeble flapping wings
Of your own tumbling thoughts

Wake up gentle lady
There is no need to sleep
I can show you a nightmare
In daylight
I can show you horror
With my living breathing flesh
Blood and bones
It's all here in my lifetime
Though I'm only yet young
I have seen it
And live it
And my life has only
Just this moment
Begun.

A Song of Circles

Sing a song of circles
Dance a spinning web of time
Heal all the scars I have
Inside my heart and on my mind

With spider hands of gentleness
Bind me in bonds of love
Let all around me speak in light
And out of darkness move

I have a song to sing of beauty
Pure and simple, fond and true
Let the song be sung in gladness
Made of me and born of you

Take my hand my gentle angel
Hold it close and let it know
All the love you have inside you
Let it feed now, let it grow

Somewhere in the sudden sunshine
I can see a darkness there
Close your golden wings around me
Keep me safe and peaceful there.

With love. . . R

With a wish that I could make some of
the things I have done invisible.

When you're not there
I live with myself
In a world of
Carefree irresponsibility

When you're not there
I laugh with the women
Of my fates path
That love me

When you're not there
The days are bright
With the sunshine
Of the good souls
Who are my friends

When you're not there
I have a freedom
To be irresponsible
To no one but myself

When you're not there
I stay awake all night
And listen to Cream records
On high fidelity stereo record players
In expensive apartments of
Passing acquaintances

When you're not there
Drinking whisky
And smoking cigarettes
Sitting in the same place
For a week

When you're not there
I have no purpose

When you're not there
I miss you

When you're not there
I love you

When you're not there

Roses are red
    they tell me
Violets are blue
    they tell me
Sugar is sweet
    they tell me
And so are you
    they tell me

———————

I don't know you
    Well do I
I don't know you
    Well at all
I don't know you
    Will be my person
I don't know you
    Have found your match
I don't know you
    Are feeling lonely
I don't know you
    Miss me much
I don't know you
    Want me always
I don't don't know you.

How can you melt me
How can you touch me
How can you teach me
When you're only half-way there
How can you promise
To fulfil my dream
How can you try to dare
I'm only a flower
That bends in the breeze
And shelters under a wall
How did I know
When I opened my head
That I can't survive here at all
Do you know where I am
Do you know what I mean
Do you honestly properly care
How can you know me
And do what I want
When only you're half-way there
My heart and my head and my hands
Are all full with you
And your life and your time
You could just fill a thimble
If you tried very hard
With everything you've got of mine.

The darkened hours of yesterday
Come creeping back as if to say
You've done it and you seem to've done it wrong.
The hours that you took to grow
Have all seemed longer long ago
And now you're standing left without the choices.
The men and sisters grown with you
Have somehow faded from the view
And sometimes you can barely hear the voices.

———————————

Song to Tommy

Tommy can you hear me shout from outside
Does my voice carry through the thick white wall
Or is it lost in the silence of searchlight beams
And bangles of barbed wire.

Tommy you can write your name
You could write it on the sky
If you could walk in freedom
Beneath it.

*To anyone who loves me enough
to read to the end.*

I AM BECOMING annoyed and impatient with this world of beer and black pudding, fried haddock and bingo, the noisy upper saloons of double decker buses and the running constantly up against the jaunty coldness of the average friendly local inhabitant who has almost no sensitivity at all.

I am slowly becoming intolerant of that typical characteristic of 'there is no place like here', not that they have ever tried anywhere else. But no matter where you come from, they want you to feel the same sort of dependence on the area, the same pride in place. It's sickening. Transfer these people out of their cell and show them the wonders of creation, and they are unmoved. Lost in a strangeness that they would never relax into and discover, like a snail who retires into the shell on his back at the first sign of danger.

My only friends here are perhaps sunshine and darkness for they carry with them on their daily visits to me a wonderful store of fantastical memories.

I am reminded whenever the sun is on my face of the last time it shone when something beautiful happened to me, of all the times it has shone, and the calm and peacefulness I always associate with sunshine, and the loneliness of darkness who is by no means a stranger to me now although I am still afraid sometimes of his power. He makes me happy too sometimes when I look through him to the moon shining down, white and icy, that cool crisp fresh peace that moonlight has. And darkness too brings sleep and peace in dreams. Dreams where anything is possible: to fight wars and win, to dance, to sing, to have every world and all worldliness at your feet, to sleep perchance to slide back into the womb and become an everlastingly impenetrable foetus. Safe from the sweet misery of life? Perhaps.

I am trying so desperately in my lifetime to find complete peace. Not oblivion, I am not trying to shut out the cruelty that is a part of any life. But I have not yet retained or maintained a core of peaceful, tranquil strength through any of the pressures I have been under. I must find myself in relation to another total complete beautiful person whom I consider is on my waveband and who is sympathetic to my kind of passion for living and can understand and share my vision. Am I asking too much? Is all the vision I have just vapour of fantastic imagination or is what I am striving for a real concrete obtainable product?

I wish I had arrived at where I am going and had made my discovery. Then perhaps I might be capable of carrying the burden of someone else's happiness and complement their existence by making it happy and complete.

I can do no more than I've done
I can say no more than I've said
I can only go now
I can only bow out gracefully
I can only leave you alone
To yourself
And your friends
I have only my world to live inside
I have only myself on the outside
I can only ask you to come in with me
See what it's like to be me
Find out what it is to be free
And easy with me
I've only got a lifetime to live
I've only got a lifetime to give
I only want to share it with you
Show it to you
Through me
And baby I can do no more.

Last Summer

A poem unfinished. . . .
> *. . . . as I hope it always will be*

Who is this who holds my body
    In her strange unselfish arms
She tries so hard to be all women
    Past and future all unknown
She does not know I walked in Heaven
    Saw the gates of Eden part
Lived and loved and talked with angels
    Carried in an angel's heart

Every eagle flies
    Why not me?

With love. . . R

How Many Deaths Do I Have To Die Before I Can Live With The Angels?

What will I find when I open my mind
Will it be what I want it to be
Will I show myself what I wish to see
Or will I cry at the sight of my blood
I have had fleeting glimpses into my soul
I have sometimes seen under my skin
But I have never been able to hold what I see
In my hand
Much less can I give it to you

Goodbye my Miranda my spirit of life
Goodbye to the sun and the stars
Goodbye all my yesterdays
Goodbye all tomorrow days
I wish I was me and not you.

With love. . . R

Ashes to Ashes

When the wind blows free
Across the purple moors
I stop to think of the world
Of the great outdoors
Where men fight for the smallest things
Where there is much room for hate
And where torture and suffering
Are not thought on until such time
As is too late.

But when can it be
Too late to think of death
That heartache and suffering
Are no longer thought on on this great earth.

Soon there will be peace
But there will be no King
Because man, to attain world peace,
Will destroy every living thing.

Play me the song of Stanley
Said the wide man with the boot
Let tears of sadness from my bright eye fall
And let me live his death again
So gentle did the minstrel play
That all around is silence
His words hung softly on the walls
And all around is silence
He took his lover to his breast
Stared into her coal black mind
But all he saw was burning fire
Of his eyes shining back.

A room with one window
A friend across the hall
Green and yellow paper
Staring from the wall
A light bulb hangs down stark and cold
Lino on the floor
A prisoner in my loneliness
Of four walls and a door
Darkness creeps on steadily
Forcing out the light
The struggle goes on quietly
And soon we're into night
Drip plip pip of a water tap
A cough through muted wall
From warm in bed and cosiness
The friend across the hall
I cry out in a silent scream
My forehead damp and cold
Finger nails crushed into palms
I'm trying to keep hold.

A song of sorrow and of love . . .

Lose you now I've found you and my
garden doesn't grow.

Dance around a pretty flower
Spinning dreams of what could be
Walk through autumn's falling silence
Break the chains and let me be

I want to wake with you around me
Golden hair on naked breast
Sleep your peace, let all be gentle
All be calm and I can rest

I don't want their paper roses
I don't want their paper sky
I want the wings of your true loving
Take my hand and see me fly.

We can walk through cracking thunder
Flashing lightning, freezing rain
We can find a summer sunshine
If your love finds me again.

With love. . . R

Your shadow that was on the floor
Goes with your smile behind the door

———————————

On the one hand it's the secret
On the other it's the pain
The insect and the candle
That dies inside the flame
But there's no sense in failure
And not much use in fear
And there's not much use in lying
When it's only you who hears.
It's your life of sprinkled bathsalts.

L IFE STARTED in the Summer of 1962 and ten years
had brought it to this point. The years of question-
ing and fear Briccha had pushed through swelled in
him a pressure of joy and escape in the slow easy tears
that rolled gently down his shiny face.

His childhood had been on the outside quite un-
eventful. His parents simple uncomplicated
working-class people with no particular ambition
except perhaps to move slightly away from their own
childhood. He had been brought up well, allowed the
freedom to choose whatever path he wanted to follow,
made to explore his personality and the personality of
others. He had struggled through his childhood clum-
sily; a shy boy with only imagination to escape into
whenever he felt lonely. He always felt a little apart
from the rest of the world. Sometimes he thought he
was perhaps the only one in it. Always more intelli-
gent than he was given credit for by his masters and
elders, he drifted through lack of encouragement
further and further into his own mind. He stopped
putting forward his ideas and lived in a world of
dreams and fantasy.

He developed an interest in painting around the
age of eleven. Nurtured and coaxed by an eccentric art
mistress at school, he practised his skill. He could
reproduce objects effectively, even achieve likenesses
of his friends in the class, but somehow, apart from the
praise, this did not satisfy him. He became an artist.
He was perhaps the first twelve-year-old eccentric the
school ever had. He devoted all his time and energy to
being, or becoming, a better artist.

The first pangs of puberty had made the rift between him and his environment greater. He no longer spoke the same language as his fellows. He moved in a world of beauty and love and of being and seeing and could not communicate any of his thoughts through words. His only language was his painting. He knew he could paint the world on a postage stamp but could only wait for it to be recognised. He had invented a language that no one yet understood. One day there would be someone who could interpret the sounds he made with paint. One day his images would be heard and the secret cat of life would be out of the bag. The great ones, the masters, were his friends and comforters. He would talk to Rembrandt and Blake and Renoir.

When he was seventeen he entered art college and found himself alone once more in an articulate world he knew nothing about. He found more and more that he was required to explain verbally what he had meant by certain gestures, and if he couldn't that meant he had no reason; that his talent was raw and naive. How could he say what he meant? If he could say it there would be no need to paint it – he would write it down. Can an inarticulate Christian explain the feeling of the presence of the Prince of Peace in his body? Can he explain the meaning of happiness and the essence of truth? Briccha could with his paintbox, but not with his mouth.

It hurts your heart
And softens your soul
When you see a man
Die

Long before
Even before
Only before
He's old.

I remember you as you were small
I remember you as you were a little bird
I don't ever think of the eagle that flies
On through the skies and kills
Take hold of your fingers and count them
You're half-way to heaven when you've found them

Know how your bones grow
Know where the blood flows
Know I am yours and not mine

In a black hour
of his sleep's loneliness,
he rolled over and
stroked the belly
of his wife's
absence.

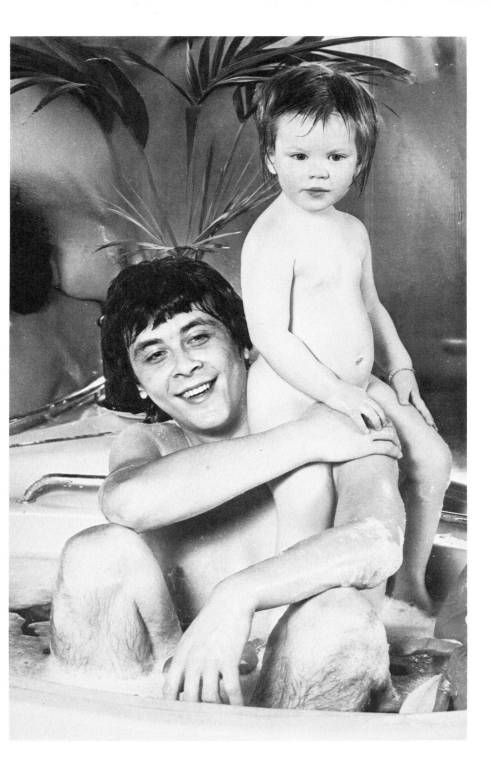

It used to be a happy room
    Full of joy and sun
Now it is an empty room
    No sign of ·anyone

One day I thought I saw myself
    Sitting on the floor
Talking to an angel
    But now I'm not so sure

No money in the meter
    No food inside the fridge
But there is damp and emptiness
    And dust on the window ledge

I'll have to scrub the walls down
    And make it all so clean
Scrape off myself from everywhere
    From everywhere I've been

I know I'll find another room
    Filled with pretty things
I'll see angels on the floor
    I'll try and touch their wings

But I love this little room
    It's safe and quiet and calm
And I know that while I'm in here
    I can't come to any harm

But I know I'll never see the angels
    Sitting on the floor
So I'll have to get away from here
    and bolt and bar the door

A Poem For Ever

I kick through the death
Of an Autumn past
Searching for dreams
That I thought would last
But nobody watered the tree

The blood has now drained
The body is dust
The soul is near dying
And die now it must
Because nobody watered the tree

I now walk through Winter
On towards Spring
To the strength of a new life
That sunshine will bring
If somebody waters the tree

I'll dig deep in the dirt
And plant a new seed
Bring everything to it
That I think it will need
And I will remember
Ah yes, I'll remember
Remember to water the tree

Baby girl widow will take care of my children
Baby girl widow will make my dreams come true

Who's June is this
Who's sky is that
What makes the world
Go round
What makes a word
Sound
What colour's black
Where's my back
How do you breathe
Where do you see winter
How do you live
When do you die
What's a question
Where's the answer
What's a line
What's the sign
What's a rhyme
And who in Hell
Is Jesus anyway.

There are fingermarks around my soul

See with your eyes, see with your eyes
Don't look too far out of sight
Feel with your hands, feel with your hands
   Don't grip too tight
   Don't forget to see
   Don't forget to see

The ground you walk on is yours
The bed you lie in is mine
All that I am is ours
All that you are is fine
   Don't forget to see
   Don't forget to see
   Don't forget me

Whenever you talk don't forget what you say
Whenever you think don't forget to pray
Whenever you recall don't forget the day
   The day you see me
   The day you see me
   The day you see me
   You will be free
   The day you see me
   You will be free
   Of me.

There Will Be A Heaven Here On Earth

Run away past promised futures
   Try to find your thoughts in dreams
All is false now all is broken
   You must
Try to get away

Shrug off thoughts of finding beauty
   With a sad and painful smile
Toss the head and breathe in deeply
   Try to get away

Crawl now into holes of darkness
   Where no light can ever be
Sleep now through the cruel hard winter
   Try to get away

The poet speaks with knives and feathers
   Pouring out his heart and soul
Trying hard to ease his darkness
   Trying hard to get away

Yet who leaves the land of Moses
   Where the earth is pure and rich
Who is he who leaves contentment
   Who will try to get away

Hear the words of youth untarnished
   When she spoke she stopped the world
Heaven is on Earth my children
   Do not try to get away

Stay and find the last beginning
   Hold it tightly to your breast
Let the life of light surround you
   There is no need to get away

With love. . . R

Sifting out slowly through cracks in the walls
Spiralling softly to earth
Floating on feathers that bend
When I breathe
I've come through
Blow the blue smoke rings out of my eyes
See them gradually fading away
The rainbows are forming high over
My head
I've come through
Let soft silken fingers play slow on
My mind.

Walk softly through the garden Mary
Ever so sweetly step
The flowers all have ears my lovely
Ever so sweetly step
They drink up April thunderstorms
Sleep softly under snow
Tell me ever so gentle Mary
How does your garden grow
With banks of painted marigolds
And blossom on lilac trees
With rambled rose and columbine
That ever so sweetly smell.

Red Saturday: *unfinished, 1979*

If you don't watch out I'm going to miss you.
My finger tips will slip
From the rim of my happiness
And I will fall stone dead, dead weight
To the knees of gloom.

The sand of a white beach
Is stained red by blood
Trickling, tickling
From my torn throat
My back has no skin
The rocks took it
And my face
I have no face
The rocks took it
Cool sea breeze
Wafts gently through
The holes in my head
Where my eyes should be
I cannot see
Sea, I cannot see
I am alive
My heart beats
My lungs fill
And slowly empty
The storm has passed
And all is calm
The sun beats down
On my bare stinging
Raw blood red flesh red
Flesh
My skin will grow again
My face is in the mirror
My eyes are in the sunlight
The sun is love
And the love is you.

A Poem

Gone before me out of my hands
Blowing like the wind
Is wasted time.

I try to catch back the breeze
But it slips through my fingers
Away round the world
While I stand
Mind still
Eyes closed inward
At the bottom of my own dreams.

Can you?

Always Be The Sunshine

I want you
To take from me
All that I can give

I want you
To live with me
The life you want to live

To find with me the happiness
To find with me the pain

To find in me fulfilment.

See the beautiful tomorrow
Through the tears of yesterday
Let a man be a man
Let him rise and let him fall
Let him cry, let him laugh
Let live a life of honesty
Let him be all he is
Let his weakness be brought close to him
Let his secret fears be known
Let him know where his strength lies
Let him know himself in relation to you
We live our lives in a mirror where
The reflection is seen through other people
And life is such that not many people
Have the time or consideration to allow
The image to be returned. That's how
We find friends and lovers.

Talk to me Julia
Sing songs of happy rhyme.
Talk to me Julia
While I have the time
To spend with you
I'm on a journey through a lifetime
I really dare not stop

On the wing of a white dove
   I sail to the calm sea
Finding love on the blue breeze
   And the sun on my hand
Blow wind for pure white
   Yellow sand come flying
Follow sunbeam softness
   And the sun on my back
Gentle through the white cloud
   Float slipping downward
Skimming on the sea rim
   Come kissing onto ground
Flapping wings of whiteness
   Fade slowly in the sky
To take one out of darkness
   And fly him to the sun.

At last I breathe
the fragrance of green tulips
through my own sense
of the beautiful
make my music
in my own ears
I look to the broad horizons
and see wonderful
amazing sights
beyond my field
of vision
At last oh God
At last.

For Judy Sunshine
and the last time I was yours.
Keep me safe inside the temple
of your memory.

The days will gently breathe
and slowly surely die.
But I will always have you
inside me.

INDEX OF FIRST LINES